Be Rich
and
Happy now!

Adam Blanche

DEDICATION

This book will help you to find a way out of
difficult financial problems, but in financial matters,
there is still a lot of difficulties.
The psychological state of many people is very difficult,
nervous state you need to put into shape!
I'll help you get back on track,
and do we cope with all the problems!

Adam Blanche

Even the worst life span after a while
it becomes a very good.

CONTENTS

Chapter 1

"Business Psychology" What do we know about this?

Looking to the rich and successful people who can not afford a lot, unlike most ordinary people inadvertently pose the question - what is the secret of their success? How should we look at life, to be able to achieve success in various affairs and thereby earn a lot of money? After all, business success is not achieved by chance, not everyone becomes rich and successful, though many try.

Psychology of business you help us to understand why is it that some people succeed in business and in life, and others do not, and that person needs to be done with them to join the ranks of the rich and successful people. In this article you will find answers to these and other questions. The first thing you need to understand each of you, dear readers, is that successful people are not born. If you will think so, then you are to limit their opportunities.

Yes, you can be born into a wealthy family, you can be born in a family of smart parents, who will be teaching your child the right things at an early age, you can be born in a rich country with great potential, get a good education and not to fight for survival, as do many people in poor countries.

But, first, it does not guarantee you success, because that is not always the children continue the work of their successful parents and do not grow so what parents want them to see, regardless of their place of birth, and secondly, the motivation to succeed at wronged life people can be much more.

The full life relaxes people and hungry, on the contrary, makes it more active, so success is best to go on an empty stomach, in my view.

Thus, the most important thing that you need to succeed in business - it is a good motivation. Strictly speaking, the motivation required for any success at all in any business.

Unmotivated man - a vegetable that does not want to do anything. Without proper motivation, you do not waste your time, not to get all sorts of knowledge, not on trying to create a business, not on something else.

Motivation - is the most important thing in business and in life.

Look at the business, at least for large, even for a small - the same fans of the business. They so much want to succeed in that case, which involved that are ready day and night they engaged in solving many different problems.

And when you are doing something all the time, with desire, with passion - you will inevitably seek to achieve this success.

However, in this case, you can become a slave to the business and significantly limit their horizons, but that's another side of the coin, we are with you, dear readers, how else will discuss separately.

So, one of the most important tasks facing the psychology of business, it is a person's motivation to achieve your goals, risk, because the risk is inevitable in

business, the ability to overcome difficulties and overall success.

The person should be unhappy with his current position in society, their financial situation, their capabilities, and himself, he should want more to begin to make the necessary efforts to achieve this more.

And if a man is satisfied, then it will not strain for some success there, some business, he will be content with what he has.

In general, as it may seem strange, but not all people are motivated money. Therefore, businesses want to do is not all. By themselves, all need money, because that way our world by these rules he lives, that without money it is almost impossible to survive. People need money to live, but not all people are willing to live for the sake of money.

And when it comes to business, the vast majority of cases, to the business flourished - they need it to live. It is only the largest businesses can afford to enjoy life without spending too much time on your business, the majority of the business always has to solve some related to their business problems. Well, in some countries, the business and did have to survive.

A survival - it is not life.

4

So the money most people, of course, will not give up as necessary to the life of the resource, but for them to engage in business, not many are ready.

But money alone does not come, the wealth of the sky does not fall down on your head, you need to strain to secure a good life. Consequently, it is necessary to have a good motivation to do business, otherwise, you can not even be put into it, because the elementary lazy to ruin any of your initiative. Love you money or not - does not matter. If you need them, then you have to start to deal with such cases, which allow to obtain a large amount of money. Business - one of such cases. Many businessmen live their business, not just doing it for the money, but for the soul. It is this approach allows them to achieve success in it and overcome various difficulties that business will inevitably arise.

So the desire, my friends, to be sure, and even if they themselves do not have the money so strongly attracted to you were ready for them to strain, then maybe improve the social status will be for you a strong incentive. Awaken the desire to change their lives for the better, revise, and even turn your outlook on life that you have the energy, a lot of energy to do business. Discard the old life for a new life, drop the old values, a good work, a stable salary, irresponsible life, because in the business world all this there is no room.

5

Remember, a businessman - a hunter, his desire for profit can be compared with the desire to catch prey hunter, so he must have the strength of character, have high self-esteem and be confident in yourself, and sometimes self-confident person. You see, money - it's a resource that we need to be able to win from the outside world, and this is always and at all times were engaged in real men - they pushed forward from the outside world resources for his family, for his flock, for your tribe. In our time, and women are engaged.

By themselves, the money is not worth anything - a conditional value, but they are in our world guide to essential resources. So it turns out that the money itself - it is also a resource so valuable, how high their purchasing power and how much we need them. In general, the value of money is determined by the fact that people are willing to pay for the money, do it. Therefore, having a lot of money, and you can have a lot of power. In short, to succeed in a business sense.

And it will only be able to achieve the kind of person who would be a real hunter for money, which will be a predator, ready, too, if not all, then a lot for the money. Business psychology helps a person to awaken their hunting and predatory instincts needed to counter a hostile outside world.

Nobody just give you their resources would not, moreover, there is plenty of wishing you had your resources away. And even create a successful business, you must know how to protect it, otherwise you have it taken away.

In business, as in war, we can not relax, you must always be ready for battle.

Generally itself striving for success when that success involves improving the quality of human life, as well as improving their social status in the society, the desire for greater freedom and greater opportunities.

Therefore, business psychology helps us also to find out how this or that person loves freedom. Not able to free the soul of man, content with some kind of work and modest wages, a simple housing and low social status in the society, in which the value of his life is low.

A man who does not aspire to the big money, to improve their social status and to expand their opportunities - simply do not know the taste of life, do not know the taste of freedom. After that something passionately wants, one must have an idea about it, he should understand that he wants to fanatically follow his dream. And let the majority of businessmen - is srednerangovye individuals who are forced to obey the high-ranking individuals in the face of power, yet their position in society quite comfortable and safe, if they have the necessary contacts and know how to adapt to various changes.

The businessman, no doubt, easier to meet their basic needs, than the man who runs it and who rank below him.

This means that a full-fledged person can not choose to do business and or policies because these activities allow the person to best meet their basic instinctual needs. And we all need to meet them.

Business - is a good start towards the top of the social pyramid.

And there, to be sure, life is much better than at the bottom.

Psychology of business to evaluate the possibility of a person who has decided to establish a business, before you offer him some steps needed to create it. It is necessary to find out what the problem is able to perform this man, and what does not. After all, before you start to do something, you need to find out whether a person is willing to, to engage in certain activities or not. And if he's not ready for it, you should find out what is required in order to prepare him properly for this activity.

You can not throw a soldier into battle unprepared, otherwise it will just be cannon fodder on the battlefield and kill him quickly. That of a man who from childhood prepared for slave wage labor, it is impossible at one time to make a successful businessman. And most of us is prepared to wage labor, we are not prepared to manage other people, and to subjugate other people, we planted a slave mentality.

And this slavish infection in the head and in the human soul, it is necessary to burn with a hot iron before you try to make it a businessman or even something more.

That's the psychology of business and do just that - it vyleplivaet from any person of a successful businessman.

And the fact that with proper operation of the person from it is possible to fashion, almost everybody, no doubt, because the adaptive abilities of the person are very high, especially if he is young.

I believe that the ability to raise their social status and learn how to earn a lot of money and make your life freer, be sure to take advantage of any reasonable person. No matter how old you are, no matter how much, you can still change your life for the better if you put your trust in professionals and let them save you from the slave units, which do not allow people to achieve great success in this world.

This world, in the form in which it currently exists, does not need successful people in large numbers - it needs the mind minded performers, slaves, through which successful people and successful. But you should not care about it, you do not have to think about the needs of the world, you should think about themselves and their needs. After all, if you do not think about themselves and do not take care - no one will think of you and does not care.

It is particularly important to invest time and money in their children so that they, unlike many of us, lived a life of freedom that they did not obey the orders of someone else, like trained dogs, but have done so, they themselves see fit to do.

Keep in mind that people can adapt, no matter how many years it was not as if they have not been rested - they can change, but only if they themselves would wish to change. Of the children can mold anyone that even insecure artist-loser, though self-confident and successful in life a man who knows what he wants and knows how to get it.

9

Any failure can be turned into a promising personality that will start your way to success with a simple business, and finish of the activity, which will have time to grow in his life.

 We could also make us obedient slaves, ready to serve the interests of others in spite of his natural instincts, and then the reverse process is possible, and then you can make a slave of man. It is clear that human learning at an early age is a thousand times easier than when he was grown up and matured as a person.

But no one says that the last failure, you can easily make a great leader or a very wealthy businessman, but who knows, all because of the desire of man depends on how hard he would work on himself.

However, a failure may cease to be a failure, it may cease to be a person with low self-esteem, self-doubt.

He can become a promising person, capable of achieving some success in life, thanks to the proper operation of the other.

With the help of business psychology, people can qualitatively change themselves, to understand their lives and by identifying feasible actions it is called, to cling to the success. So those of you who do not want to put up with their situation in life, this opportunity, I believe you need to use. In the end, you lose, except time and money that you and since you have something to spend. So it is better to let it be something your active attempt to become those whom you do not be ashamed to look in the mirror.

Chapter 2

"Savings" Why do we need it?

For each of us, the economy is perhaps the most common word we hear everywhere. Is it important to save?Live frugally, a longing many would say whether the deal to buy new clothes. Gadgets and the like. This is life!Has your global recession or not, you will surely come in the handy knowledge of how you can save money and how to spend them skillfully. Recently it has been observed that in some countries, the amount of interest for 10 years exceeded deposited amount of money. Of course, today not many banks offer are not as good conditions and interest from investments is not always as high as investors had hoped. As if that was not wise to have some savings for emergencies. Before you buy an expensive item, consider whether this item is needed. Buy new things on sale or purchase good used items. Smallpox and Inna, who live in Norway, wanted to buy a stroller for his son Dany. They managed to find a new wheelchair for almost half the cost.

Smallpox says: "I am sure that when Danny grows up, we will be able to sell it at a good price." But he warns: In order to find the right offer, takes time.Do not make impulsive decisions, first how to think. If you do think that something you need, try to look for something similar in the discount centers, or second-hand stores. In addition, you can save, if you do not chase the brand name. Instead of buying the latest models of children's clothes at expensive stores, why not take the things that you have given friends or relatives?

For infants, you can use cloth diapers to be washed. In disposable diapers for two years you'll spend around $ 3,000 or more. The cloth diapers for the same time will cost you 250-300 dollars. Modern cloth diapers easy to use, and from less damage to the environment! Remember that usually cheaper to buy food and prepare meals themselves than to dine in the cafe or restaurant. Teach children to cook. Instead, of expensive soft drinks is better to drink water, the healthier and cheaper.

Not so long ago, almost all families had their own vegetable garden. Do not you grow something yourself? Many citizens living in apartments or small houses, finding a place to put anything. It's amazing how much you can grow on a small plot of land! Using a mobile phone call on it only if necessary. This is better to allocate a certain amount of negotiation and make it to the account. If you have a clothes dryer, then why not use it less often? Some washed clothes or even the whole you can just hang out to dry.

And how often do you turn on the air conditioner or heater? Ask yourself: "Is it true that the weather is such that there is a need?" You can also ask others how they are able to spend less energy. Besides practical open a savings account at the bank. As the saying goes, do not put all your money in one pocket. It happens that the banks and other financial institutions to fail. I have experienced. " Therefore, it is better to choose a bank, and which deposits are insured by the state.

Paying credit card debts or any loans, try to pay a monthly amount above the set minimum. First, focus on the repayment of debt with the highest payout percentage. Restates habit overspend, it is especially important. Beware of greed, live within your means and be happy with it!

Rarely who have the ability to immediately pay the full cost of a house or apartment. Therefore, many take out a bank loan. Then the monthly payments the bank can be regarded as payment for rent. And when the bank paid the entire amount, the house becomes the property of residents.

Many profitable take a loan to buy an economy car. The sooner the people will pay the loan, the more likely the vehicle will turn their valuable possessions - which is also a kind of way of accumulation. Some belief visionary buys a used car in good condition and with a relatively low mileage. Other save by using public transport or bicycle.

In any case, when shopping, be reasonable, realistic and weighted decisions are made. Thoughtless spending can become addictive and cause a lot of troubles. But caution and prudence - the key to prosperity. In addition, the ability to properly manage the money can be very useful. The global economic crisis has shown how important it is to live according to a well-calculated budget. What is the budget?

It estimates of income and expenditure of a person, family, company or state. In the preparation of the budget should involve all domestic, to take responsibility for each media family. From time to time members of the family should be together to discuss how to implement their plans. Creating a family budget is good for everyone because everyone learns to live without departing from the established framework. Some make a budget, using a computer program. Others do it with a pencil in his hand: they share the list Leah columns: income and expenses. In addition, each kneading and is planning a certain amount on annual expenditures, such as income tax and holidays.

Test Methods - to lay the money on the envelope marked "Power". "Rent." "Transport". "Electricity". "Treatment" and the like.

People used to put in such monthly cash envelopes. Now many believe it is safer just to make money on the bank account and spend them as needed. If the salary is transferred to the bank account, then it should be how to allocate the money, not less important. For example, if you lack the funds deposited in the kneading of the meat does not need to spend those designed for savings.

There is more happiness when a person gives another time, effort, and some of his money, he feels happier. At the beginning of the article mentioned three ways how to manage money. The money saved up to the fact that they usefully spend. The most intelligent and the best way to dispose of money - share them.

First of all think about the relationship, the important events in your life, that you helped someone and not about money and things.

If you are trying to help those who are less fortunate, while kindness and generosity will return to you with interest. But most importantly - you will feel the joy because he helped his neighbor.

Giving brings happiness!

Chapter 3

«Hold successful people»

You have no idea how important in your life, playing environment around you. From what people will be with you throughout your life, will depend on your whole life, but you also play a huge role in who is around you. Surely you've heard the saying, "Who lead the, from, and rack up" - this is a very wise saying that one hundred percent of the work. Parents, we do not choose, because our childhood depends precisely on them, but when we grow up, we are able to identify those who will be around us. If you want to live a happy and full life colors, you surround yourself with whiners and losers, as it is impossible. Such people take our energy, they chop us wings, take away our enthusiasm, suppress our psyche. Do not communicate with such people, keep successful people, cheerful and optimistic.

16

Communicating with people who never lose heart, constantly striving for more and always see the opportunities rather than problems, you charge them with energy, feel a surge of strength, feel life and its significance in it. You need only look at the success in the life of a man who you think the idea to see your affinity with him. You will see that it is the same as you, fashioned out of the same of what you do, the only thing that distinguishes it from you, it is a higher confidence. You see, you can cry and hope for the fate that has not brought you happiness on a plate with a golden platter, but you can build your own happiness, to seek and find success. World of losers - is the dead swamp, it is an absolute liability, without any hope for the best. And it's not people have born losers, it has made them such laziness. There is nothing that we could not fix it, even the mistakes of nature, man is able to turn into a victory. Just look at people with disabilities from birth, not on those who complain about their fate, and those who have achieved certain results in your life who does not give up and resigns himself to his fate. Do not they inspire us, not we to hands and feet, can not complain at this life, where we have so many opportunities? Of course there is, of course, we all can and should do everything we can to make the world around us was perfect.

Only losers and whiners only negative mood melancholic can find a lot of reasons to kill any enthusiasm in us.

17

Throw them away, or you can run from these people, their negativity is contagious, their nagging kills, kills in us human, all-powerful and can do anything.

If you plan to live a decent life, if you want to reach their full potential, keep successful people hold those who see possibilities rather than problems, learn from them and emulate them, without losing their individuality. Communication with only one successful person, positively charged to live, give you a tremendous amount of energy, thanks to which you will be able to get the ball rolling, and further accelerate. Charges themselves and charge the other, remember, people do not know that it is something can not until he did not tell about it. Be with those who do not know that there are impossible things, because there are none, only the tasks that you need to solve. Wherever you are, look for strong people and be with them, your surroundings make you, and you decide what will be your environment. So do not be surprised that you are a loser if you are around the same failures, and it suits you. Fall, much easier than to get up and lift the other, it requires incredible effort. Losers and weaklings, pulling us down, to themselves, and they get it, it's so easy to relax and go with the flow. But strong people to help them rise to the level that is much more difficult, especially if you do not want to. And to want to climb, it is necessary first of all to give up life on the bottom, do not blame anybody for it but himself, and it does not justify. Your position in life reflects your essence, you can always change.

18

Remember, people are not born successful or failures, they choose the path that will be used in this life. And the choice is always possible to change, no matter how many years you have not been, and no matter what life you have not lived. The path of successful people is the way of strong and responsible, having entered it, you can not afford weakness, you do not get to look guilty because everything will depend on you. This is the way decent people who can rightfully call himself a man. As hard as it is to you was not, keep successful people, all possible methods, try to join their team, if you're not in it for himself put it the main goal. If you stick with the winners, you will also win, it's very important, trust me, your life is highly dependent on your environment, efforts are being, that it is worthy of you, and you accordingly it.

Chapter 4

«True desire»

The true desire of man, first of all, are directly related to its adequate perception of the world in which he lives, if a person looks at life as it is, in fact, all his desires are natural, if it's something blinds or what kind of naturalness and can be no question. A modern man blinded by a lot, so the question of the truth of a desire for a person aware of his own blindness is quite acute. Adult, the adequate and more or less conscious person who is not afraid of responsibility - does not want to be manipulated. He who does not want to bear any responsibility for himself, much less for other people, not just susceptible to manipulation, a man he wishes to him and his desires manipulated. This is a key moment, in this article, we have in this matter. After all, the responsibility has adequate people with a sober outlook on life, and only such people - sober-minded, can have a really true desires and not inspired by someone else.

20

And if a person does not want to take responsibility for their lives, and then to wonder about which of his desires are true and which are not, it is probably not worth it. For what it matter who and how to manipulate them, if he wants to.

In true desires have two powerful roots, which speak of the truth of what really may want to man. Firstly, given the perception of what a man of peace, his desire to be formed in the context of the time in which one lives, and reflect the environment in which it is located. Silly, you see, to desire, what I do not have a clue and do not understand the meaning and consequences of his desire. At the same time, pushing its foundation in natural needs, which I hope you all know, the human desire to become a vital necessity. Here, just as without air, food and water, a person can die, so by all means, he will seek to satisfy their need for air, water and food, as well as any other desired, it must be based on a vital necessity.

If we do not do that - then everything, then death, nowhere to retreat, or you got what you want, or you lose in this game called life. This is our first root, which has drawn little roots that affect our psyche and to some extent feed off our desires, but the root rests on the vital need - basic. It is a matter of life and death does not stop the man in front of a variety of life's difficulties on the way to the fulfillment of its desires.

It is understandable, because "life instinct" is as relevant as the conscious and subconscious level, it is a strong stimulus to growth, it is not blind faith - it is a vital necessity.

The root of the number two - it is our ego, and with it, a thorough understanding of the man, who he is and what are its features. In any case, it is possible our understanding, to which we are able to come. And here the question is about the psychology of the person, and his conscious perception of life, the less awareness, the greater the role of the human ego is the root of the number two, and the more awareness, the correspondingly greater understanding of the role in the makeup of the true desire of man. Let me explain what I mean, but let's start from afar. I once read a book about how a strong desire to be a man, if he is not driven by the need and duty and desire. The author wrote about the power of words: "I want" in comparison with the word "necessary". And I am with him completely in that agree to will certainly stronger than all these "must" and "must", but it is not the strongest and most powerful stimulus, and most importantly, that the superficial, emotional wanting a man of anything, can be very far from the truth what he really wants. But the word "do not want", that is a very strong reluctance to anything that's really a powerful incentive for the true desire of man. Negativity in our lives, there is no accident, it is a source of information from the outside world, which comes to an unconscious most of the human mind, and let a person can not understand something, but can feel.

Feel the shit we all can, and it can stir us, get first to grow in life, and secondly to act, that is, not to be passive.

I do not know who invented this world, but everything in it is set to rise on the motion, energy. And the desire of man more natural than it is more aimed at the growth of the person and its development. Well, that is: "I want"? Is the force, given the unconsciousness of the majority of people and their susceptibility to manipulation?

Yes, it's a match, which is very fleeting, faced with the first difficulties of life. Desire is based on emotions, it has the same life expectancy as the emotion itself, on which it was founded. But desire, based on the reluctance of clinging ego unconscious person strong enough to he raised his ass and began to act, embodying that desire a reality. The truth is it should be noted that a person has developed immunity to the negative, we're such creatures that get used to everything, and even pecking us in the ass "roasted rooster," often it is absolutely indifferent, and only the already quite appalling situation, forcing people to act.

That's when a man has born a true desire, the number one feed on the roots, that rests on the vital need and reflects the natural need of man and clings his ego, in this case, write the word with a capital letter, it is hard.

I want a house - that of course you may want to, maybe even very much and all my life, and so it and not get hold.

23

But for example - do not want to live in a communal apartment as hell
know who this is harder, and here the desire to thoroughly annoying
brain, causing the person to improve their living conditions. You see
friends, to desire to have a home, but do not have the capabilities to it -
do not wish so, to think that you will. And if you have, instead of the
house - a goat, it's not about your opportunities, ostensibly mismatched
with your desire to speak, but the tuhlosti your desire, enough for only a
goat. The true desire may be implemented either in time or stay in the
process of implementation, given the fact that we do not live forever,
and life is not always adapts to our ambitions.

It is - the desire can not be born and dead in the human mind, if it is
present, it dies with the man. It may not be patted on his tongue or a
maximum - to express it in his sluggish and hesitant actions that resting
in the early difficulties were entirely man stopped. Such a person does
not want anything, and his desire is not true. And even if such a person
achieve something in life, driven by its "hochushkoy" it will certainly
not be the most outstanding results. The sweetness of the carrot is
always less effective than the pain of the whip, to which even can be
used to, but the pain at rest, the person will not leave.

Linking I wrote at the beginning, with a consistent presentation of all
I have described aspects of human behavior in the formation of his
various desires, we'll come to understand that a person does not need
much, actually. However, circumstances force us to want more, life
itself demands from us this because it is arranged so that it is necessary
to play actively.

24

But as man's awareness of who he is and what his possibilities,
which I mentioned, in fact, is to overlay all the above.
That is, we take into account all that we have in our life, and
with the understanding of ourselves as beings capable of
everything, if we take responsibility for themselves, want exactly
what is included in the extent of our interests with the full
understanding of the need for us cheat or. What our ego is born
reluctance to anything or anyone that our needs have acquired
the form needs to be the most convenient way to satisfy their
need for that time and circumstances around us, putting the final
form of our desire on the foundation of the vital importance of
all it should be fully understood by us.
If you do not understand something in his desire, if you can not
relate it to me described incentives that should be your desire to
nurture and make it real, while not in a hurry to want something
and for something to strive for. It is better to think about the fact
that you do not want that in this life is not drawn as you need and
try to justify their desire, that this stimulus. False desire to
impose on you, now much many, these desires are so weak that
people even offer to implement them by taking a loan, in order to
hot to you and totally unconscious in understanding his desire,
how quickly it performed at the behest of a magic wand.
But if the life you will secure to the wall, this is when it will put
you in front of a choice: either to live or act, that act according to
circumstances, deliberately and with meaning, rather than

reacting to external stimuli, so then you wake up the true desire that you understand it is as true, I remember my words. After all, I can not write much here, just playing with words that may awaken in you an understanding of the true desire, but can not do so, because the knowledge base and understanding of the people can be very different. So pay attention to the negativity around you, because he, unlike words, talking to a person in another language and gives him clearly understand and feel what he may actually want.

To test yourself something is always better than in theory than to know. Well, as I, in turn, probably will finish this topic, and let there are plenty of aspects that we would do well to analyze under the understanding of the truth of our desires, I think it is better to leave for later. My observations show that too great articles difficult to read people, so now I will try to write shorter. But finally, I'd like to ask each of you dear readers a question of the next character, so you can see how you could get to the core of what I wrote. So, imagine that you have caught a goldfish, which will fulfill all your desires. We will not contact you to focus on the amount of these desires, the number does not matter. It may be - three wishes, ten, a hundred and desires, not the number of business desires, and a man who understands either itself or not. So the question is: what will you ask of a goldfish? Think carefully, do not rush to their answers, and do not rush to his wishes, as I said, it is important to think, there is no limitation in the desires, one desire or a million desires, great value it has.

26

Read the article if you need more time, and then begin to think,
decide that you will ask the goldfish. Well, I hope you followed
my call to think, because now I'll tell you about that, I began to
ask the goldfish. And I would have nothing she did not ask
anything at all, even if there was not a stitch, I would have just
let go of, so to say, stronger than her desire to live, is so strong
that she even wanted to bribe me, my wishes. If I did, there was
a desire, not by my thoughts, but by circumstances not connected
with the question of life and death, it would not be true desires. It
would be a manipulation by me through external stimuli, makes
me weak and dependent. The true desire will never have the urge
to the outside world, you never have anyone, except themselves,
do not ask if you really want something. Neither God nor the
president nor the mom and dad can not give you what you really
want, and they can not do that because you are so strong and
free, if you are, something actually wants, you will get it through
their own efforts.

Other people, you can just buy and buy, they not only your
desire and your freedom with your desire, make you weak and
dependent. Friends, when I wrote you not understood, do not
worry, go to page a free consultation and email me what you do
not understand on this article, write your opinion about it. And
please, if you wanted something goldfish, write to me about it,
honestly.

Do not pay attention to my words about my behavior, write me about their thoughts and their understanding of life. After all, your desires are important, in terms of their analysis and understanding of their nature. Contact friends, I need to know whether you understand me or not. And if I do not explain if you do not understand me, then I will take into account the mistakes in future articles. It will make my job more productive, and that you and I will benefit.

Chapter 5

«Attitude to money»

Most importantly, what we should pay attention, studying the psychology of money and the money itself, it is our to them for money, the attitude. As I said above, it can be different, and this depends on our attitude to money, especially from those beliefs that we hold. And these our internal beliefs are formed in our country, mainly on the basis of the beliefs that are held by people around us and they inspire us. We ourselves, having come into the world completely clean and empty, nothing about money do not know and can not know. Money for us means nothing as long as we do not face them directly. As they get older, we gain the knowledge and experience the world around us, teaches and educates us in a certain way. And depending on the specifics of our training and education, as well as the environment in which we live, we have formed the corresponding fundamental outlook on life and on the money, and along with those of overt and covert rules and laws under which they operate.

Think about the source of your fundamental knowledge about money. Remember who and how for the first time to tell you about them? Pay attention to the environment in which you grew up and in the attitude of others, and the people around you about money. Here, all this knowledge and the people who surround you is that basic, which formed your own attitude to money. It you can be adequate to reality, and can be far from it. How realistic are your views on money, the easier it will be to earn them, and most importantly, the more stable is your internal state, an excess or shortage of money.

We all know that, depending on whether or not a person has money, his behavior may be different. The same person can behave differently depending on how much he presently money. For example, a bankrupt person may fall into severe depression and may even commit suicide because of the loss of a certain amount of money, which of course is a very stupid decision, but people, unfortunately, are able to accept it. In another case, a man can suddenly become rich and because of this has changed dramatically, as a rule, not for the better. Therefore, they say that money spoils people. All this psychological instability affects human behavior is the result of just the same inadequate man's relationship to money, which does not, he manages the money, and the money they manage.

Generally, money, psychology, and that the relationship that exists between them is, in fact, the relationship of the spiritual world to the material world. And when money changes a person, there is a merge of the material world to the spiritual world.

That is, the money being material value, in spite of their inherent in the ideological sense, affect our immaterial essence, the spiritual essence of man, thus showing us the clear relationship between the material and immaterial world.

Conversely, changing the internal, qualitative changing, people can significantly improve their financial situation, which again indicate that very relationship. You know what that means? This means that with adequate regard to money, you put it in the first place itself as a money earner, as a person who thanks to his personal qualities, is able to make any necessary amount of money to him. No money should give you confidence and your self-confidence should lead you to money, too big money. After all, man is not a thing, and the money and that person must manipulate this thing, not a thing to be manipulated.

Effect of money per person is carried out by the influence of money by some people on the other. On their own money or they can not affect a person because they do not have any goals, money - it's just a tool. But people have goals that they achieve by this tool, we buy our time, labor, knowledge, we produce the material values and our respect and even our love.

All that we are willing to sell for money, we can buy. And when we take the money, as something separate and independent, we can not help noticing how this money for us to buy with all the giblets, and also harm us.

Well, for example, how to fight for the money, as much as possible for them to kill and to risk their lives?

A normal person, adequately relating to money, this idea has never occurred to not come out of despair, he even would not trade my life and it would not kill for the money of other people. Life is priceless, life - priceless. We need to understand this. We, most of us, unfortunately, is too mediocre in this matter, too unreasonable, we do not understand, how should we relate to money. It turns out that the money is not controlled by us, through our attitude towards them, and other people govern us, in its sole discretion, when they buy us. So think about who is currently manipulating you, forcing you to serve him for the money, and whether it is possible such that you, and not you, could someone to buy and thus achieve their goals?

We need to decide what is more important for us in this life - we, or money. We need to define the role of money, which they will perform in our lives, thereby indicating to them - their place. Will they be for us a tool with which we can achieve their goals, or they will be a goal to which we will strive all his life, going for a carrot like donkeys? With this, each of us must decide. But in any case, the role of money will always be secondary because the money is just an idea, tool, symbolic value in which we all believe and just so in varying degrees obey the idea.

32

However, it is important to understand the psychology of money
it is, in fact, human psychology, irrational man who seeks good,
seeks to power tends to assert themselves, to ensure that take
place in this life as a person, to be better than others, to subjugate
the will of others. Money helps a person to come to all of this.
And he understands that. On a subconscious level, it connects
people money so good with the happiness which he so badly
needs and which he pushed his instincts. The fact that money
itself is earned by certain knowledge and skills, due to certain
personal qualities, a man of little interest.

Many people do not care about the reason, allows to get the
money, they are often interested in the investigation, that is, the
money itself. Because of the inadequate attitude of some people
money when they do not understand that they are dealing with a
symbolic value, it is to some extent a reflection of their mental
abilities and personal qualities, many of them simply do not
know how to attract money into your life.

Warning Some people drew the psychology of attraction of
money, which can be studied to understand how to behave, how
to think and what to do to have a lot, or, in any case, a sufficient
amount of money. The need for money experienced by all, but to
extract them, do not know how many. Knowledge and skills to
help you get the money, this is a very valuable thing, having that,
you are always and under all circumstances, will be in the
money.

That is why many people want to know - how to attract money, that this should be done in a drum have to knock to get rich. But it is not only knowledge and skills, the point is still in your home state, without which you can not use your existing knowledge, will not be able to use them to get their results. That's the problem. About money really need to know much to have them. The need for such knowledge is, and knowledge itself too, but again, not enough to get them, they still need to digest, that is, to understand, and most importantly, we must be able to apply them in their lives, only then will we get them the result the form of money. But without the necessary inner attitude, it is difficult to decide on any business, it is difficult in general to do anything to something to come. In general, the attitude towards money is easier not to give them too much importance and do not use them to assess themselves and their qualities better than try to develop the best, the strongest qualities such as responsibility, perseverance, discipline, and others to come to money. The most important value in this life that you can only have - is you. And everything else, as your development, and thanks to your hard work. Learn and develop, and then a lot in this life submit to your will. For me, as a person, confronted daily with a variety of problems and solving them, it is obvious that it is necessary to study the psychology of money very seriously.

Money in our lives is very important because we constantly have to deal with them, which means we should be able to use a man's relation to the money in their own interests.

And most importantly, we have our own attitude towards them to take advantage of, we need to be able to control their emotions and not to succumb to their influence on us when we are dealing with money. And remember, the role of money, in spite of its importance, objectively, is less important than our own role in this life. If you understand this, you will gain strength, and the people who do not understand it, you'll buy for the money and use them as a resource to their advantage. So in fact, happening today, some people work for money, but in others, money is working for them. Everyone, of their own accord, something actively interested in, based on their understanding of the importance of something for him and his life. For example, people interested in the psychology of money, are interested in it, as a rule, in order to explain their own behavior and the behavior of other people who have a certain way of changing money. And rightly so, because seeing the impact of money on a person can be very successful in manipulating, which is the norm in our world, where everything is bought and everything is sold. Well, maybe, after all, not all of us can be bought and sold, not all, but nonetheless, a great deal. And most importantly, what you can buy for the money - this is definitely the man. Now let's talk about the love of money. Do I love money? In principle, yes, you. Besides, willy-nilly, but we are all in varying degrees we have to love them.

Someone who likes to spend left and right, someone who likes to save money, feeling thanks to its accumulated rich man, but someone who likes to earn them, there are such people.

Anyway, we love money, because to them we can buy all the things that we want to have, what we need and what we want to have. But love, real love is not just our use of something or someone in their own interests, it is also responsible for the fact that we love and those we love and care about something and someone. If you love a person, you do not just use it when you want and how you want, you still care about the person. You think about his well-being, you hereby assigns the responsibility for this person and do everything to ensure that this person was well with you, and you, respectively, was well with him. That is exactly the same things with the money. They, too, need to properly love them, too, need to take care of them should also be responsible and can not afford to throw them left and right. And let the money is an inanimate object, however, we must strive to ensure that the money was well with us, and then we will be well with them, because we have to be good enough, maybe even too much.

So that money can and should love, but not in order to serve them, and to respect and appreciate them. Such an attitude is important not for the money, it is important for us, money is no mystery and no real power there, they're just a thing, a tool, which we enjoyed. Such an attitude, so that's, right love of money is needed in our mind that controls our behavior.

A person who does not like money to part with them at the first opportunity, he simply spends recklessly. And, of course, such a person-spenders, is never money, unless they come to him very quickly and in large quantities. But such privileged place where you can easily earn a lot of money, sometimes even without doing anything for it, available units. Most of us have to work for money, thus appreciating the money, we appreciate your work. Most people do not know how to respectfully and lovingly refer to money, constantly go into debt because they live not through. Such an irresponsible life marred by constant financial problems, due to which many families are frequent scandals. We've all heard about that attractive force, which has love, but what is this force, know, unfortunately, not many, with the result that some people believe, first of all, the manifestation of egoism true love. But true love - it is not selfishness. True love - is, once again, taking care of those you love, and this donation is for the sake of love. Of course, I did not call you to sacrifice their health and, even more, lives for the money, but highly recommend you treat them with respect. Do not forget that every penny you earn - it's a piece of your life. You've spent most of his life in terms of time and part of Svay vital energy, in order to earn it. Well, so keep your life in the toilet, throwing their money away.

Judge for yourself how much we have to sacrifice for the sake of earning money.

We and our time to spend it, and strength, and some even their health spending out to earn money. This is a serious sacrifice friend, going to that, we will certainly demonstrate our love of money.

But what happens next? And then, we somehow did not watch that much of us leave our money earned with sweat and blood. We rarely pay attention to what the things we spend it, what services we pay for them, what is the cost of these goods and services. Why are we so quick to part with money earned us why stop loving them, once they have come from? Instead of carefully plan each of his purchase, trying to save as much of their money, we scatter them left and right as if it's not the money and some garbage.

So, you know, money is like. So, even himself and his work not like. I can understand those people who do not squander their and other people's money, for which they themselves do not work up a sweat. Such people do not care about other people's labor, and it is clear, do not mind someone else. But with their hard-earned money, you can not do that. On a primarily do so can not, you can not turn your work into the garbage in the garbage. We want to have always had money in the required amount, but it can easily part with them, contradicting thus their own desires. Think about it before you once again, to decide on any purchase of dubious importance. The money, in general, should be treated very easily, without unnecessary emotions, as if you do not the situation was with them.

No need to turn them into the meaning of his life, otherwise this very life you will not. What life can be a constant pursuit of money?

You see friends, your relationship to the psychology of money is not much different from your relationship to all other things and events in life. It is formed from your world that we all have been incomplete. No need to say upset over the fact that you, in your opinion, a little money because it is possible that in this segment of your life, that's the way it should be. We can not know exactly how good or bad for us, is our current financial situation, as it is each of us is unique. Not for nothing because Socrates said that he knew only one thing - it does not know anything because we really do not know much in this life, we just think that is something we know and understand.

It turns out that experiencing negative emotions, because of the lack of money, people do not really know how to present it, good or bad. It is possible that your current financial situation is a kind of experience that you need to purchase in order to be ready for possession of large sums of money, which is not only joy but sorrow can bring to people. So much upset because of lack of money and in general due to not enough to please you, for one reason or another, life, you definitely should not. Rejoice that you have, well, as far as possible, of course, strive for more, it is both useful and interesting.

Chapter 6

«Think positively»

If you think about the reality - it's the only perception. If you're feeling confident, the way it is. If everything goes wrong, but you do not notice it, then actually nothing is lost, right? So start to think positively! This will not be fooled. Do not think that positive thoughts - this is nonsense, because you just take matters into their own hands. If you find yourself thinking: "Oh my God, I'm so fat", stop. Paraphrase. Say it again, only, this, time thinks so: "I do not like my weight.

What do I do, to change it? "Thoughts must not only be sunny and rosy but be kind to currently still stands. Positive thinking leads to positive and more confident behavior. You know what it happens when you think about yourself in a negative way? It becomes a habit, which is why you begin to see the negative in

everything. You can start to gossip, complain or become one of those who constantly humiliates others.

Do not allow this. Be thankful. So, you have already read the article about how to think positively, but still confused? Then start with gratitude. The more events that occur in your life, you will remember, the higher the likelihood that everything will not be so bad. It is sad is that we are very easy to forget that we have! Think about it. You are alive, dressed, you have talent (what?), People who love you, and the future - and this is just basic.

This is what most people have, and that you have those things which others do not? Smile. Continuing debate about what is primary - thought or behavior. It turns out your mind the following tips in your body, so learn how to cheat the brain and smile! It turned out that smile - the muscular equivalent of oatmeal. Incidentally, the bunting - it is almost a miracle in the world of products, and here's why: When you smile, your body produces endorphin's and serotonin. If you forcing a smile, you literally become happier. You will not look happier and seemed happy - you'll be happier. Smiling relieves stress, lowers blood pressure, strengthens the immune system. how oatmeal, but without the calories and always at hand. Smiling makes us more attractive to others. Did you this had on one said?

P.S. Generally, the happier people are, the more confident they are. This is something there. No sense to worry when things are good!

A change of scenery. Think about who you are at home, who you are learning who you work, who you are at your favorite cafe. Probably not the same person, right? It is possible that in one or another situation, you feel more comfortable and confident, so if you are now in an unpleasant place for you, then get up and go!

Unfortunately, you can not just get up and go to the middle of the dinner in the diner. But the next time you feel that you are bad, think about where you are. The realization that it may be in a situation, and not in you, you have to remove the goods.

Use visualization and deep breathing. It is rather a short-term solution. If you are going to talk to the pretty boy or a speech, you can use the following methods: imagine that you are an excellent job and everything goes smoothly. If you wait for success, he can come, but if you wait for the failure, it is sure to happen. Take a deep breath. When we breathe in too fast, our heart rate increases and the brain begins to think: "fight or flight". So you're just starting to get nervous even stronger.

Since you do not have to hunt for huge mammoths in the near future, the benefits of such a reaction of the body is not. Speak with him. Look in the mirror and try to convince yourself that you are - that's you, and you are magnificent. You say to yourself that you have nothing to hide, not counting myself. Take the mirror confident and proud posture that will make you believe in them.

Dress to the nines.

42

How would you feel if it went to an expensive restaurant in their favorite pajamas with penguins, and hair refused to lie down gently? Probably, insecure and awkward. And how would you feel if logged in at the same place in their best outfit? Not clothes make the man, but it can make you feel like a million dollars.

It is much easier to like yourself if a person knows what looks good. Take a shower, brush your hair, put on clean clothes and apply perfume on your skin that will charm all around. It is not necessary to dress up as if you go to the prom but to work hard and make the image is complete.

Watch your posture. Find a room or space where a lot of people. 9 times out of 10 you will be able to determine the insecure person on track and stop or omissions view. In fact, even just copying his behavior make you feel insecure. Do not do this! Lift the chin, pull the shoulders back and walk confident gait. Remember that you always have someone watching.

Begin to play sports. When a man goes in for sports, it looks better. When a man looks better, he feels better. In addition, exercise helps release endorphin's give us a sense of productivity, are charged with energy and give us confidence. And, of course, they promote health, so we are living longer. There is no need to run a marathon to benefit from physical exercises.

43

Thirty minutes a day of sport (even if the time will be divided into small segments) will be enough. Wear bright clothing. During the mourning black clothes are not just so she it reflects the mood of the person. People have a lot of associations with flowers. If you feel sad, wear something bright. It is possible that for the confidence you do not miss only noticeable accent.

To do what you're good at. Yes, you are good at something. Even if cleaning toilets, you have it good yield. And you know it! When we do that we succeed, we feel proud and enjoy the ability to get things done. With these feelings and confidence begin. It should be as often as possible to do what it turns. This will remind you that you have done. Understanding what you're good at something, you own some skill, gives you have a special character, it gives the topic of conversation, makes you interesting in the eyes others and gives a pleasant feeling of completion. We have already said that it is also

fun? What are you waiting for? Take time for yourself and your loved ones enjoy a business. Talk to everyone. Part of insecurity due to the fact that we do not fully understand people. To avoid this, speak with everyone. Communicate with everyone, even if you just drop a note about the bus is late. Here's what you learn through this:

Most people are quite friendly. They do not want to offend or condemn you. In fact, they are likely to enjoy a chat with you, and you - to them. Most people do not like to take the initiative. They will open if you make the first step.

44

When you need to get out of their comfort zone, they are nervous
as much as you. People turn in on themselves. They are doing
what is always involved and do not like to be different. It's
boring. It is not necessary to do so. You will learn a lot from
people who do not like you.

Continue to communicate with everyone. Yes, go ahead. The
more you talk to people, the less it will scare you, the less you
will you will worry about what will think about you, the less you
will think that everything is better than you, and the more you
will realize that most people are absolutely normal. Ideal people
do not, so you have no reason to worry about how you seem to
others. The more you talk to people, the more you learn about
communication. It may scare you, but after the hundredth call
about the same. I do not know how or where to start? You can
read articles about how to be an extrovert, the soul of the
company and sociable person. Do others compliments.
Remember the positive, we were talking about earlier? It turns
out that people like it. Praise people, and they will see that you
know how to talk nice. It's like the principle of "giving more
pleasant than to receive." It's nice when someone makes you a
compliment, but still pleasant to realize that you helped someone
to see something good in itself. Learn to accept compliments. A
simple "thank you" - the best way to do it. Not red or excuses, if
someone is nice to you.

Of course, that you show your humility, but it is not good in relation to the speaker. Imagine that you gave you a gift, and you say, "No, no, I do not deserve it, leave yourself." Worse than you can imagine!

This must be sincere compliments. Do not say anything if really do not think so. Watch for yourself and everyone around you. Wherein:

Watch for yourself and others, rather than to condemn. When you stop judging others, it may take a negative. Your mind will be revealed and you will learn something new.

Watch for yourself and for others to learn. What makes others so confident? What makes you feel good about yourself and what is not? What triggers stiffness and what behaviors are inherent in you?

Find role models in real life. If you have an example to follow, you can become more confident. You need a source of positive emotions, which will give you strength when you need it. You should not only find a role model or mentor, and surround yourself with positive people. If you are often dealing with people who are trying to humiliate you (intentionally or not), or compel you to be who you are not, you will never be happy. Such communication is not worth it, no matter how much these people are beautiful, rich, or clever. Stay true to yourself. It is difficult to be confident in their abilities if you try to be someone else. It is important not only to think about what you want to appear confident, but who you really are. Get rid of unnecessary and just be yourself. So it will be much easier.

You can not be happy if you try to be someone else.

46

Perhaps the first time you will notice that people are drawn to you (thanks to the clothing that suits you, and other things), but sooner or later it will pass and you will be alone with their view of themselves. If some part of you is telling you that the image that you create - it's not you, listen to yourself. It is important to believe in yourself and do what is right for you, and then you will have confidence.

Chapter 7

«The correct attitude to money»

For the problem is not the number one in your life, they should be properly treated, they must be understood in a certain way, and then they generally will not be a problem for you, because it should not be. Personally, I realized that even before I became a lot of money, because it accelerated their rise largely, plus a significant improvement in my financial situation, as does not impact on my character and worldview. And now I'll tell you about the psychology of the person, which must be before and after he got some money, not just money, but a lot of money. I'm not going to tell you about your condition when you have no money, because if you do not have them or have them a little, you know what it is, and I am fully convinced that in this case, money is for you than - What is difficult for. It is a natural conclusion with which you surely will agree, because if they gave you to easily, you probably have them would be great, although I understand that this concept is situational, it is possible after all, on the neck of someone to sit, and it, too, will be easy money.

48

But you are talking after all about making money and disadvantages as other situations are not so important to consider them. So try to imagine even for a moment that in fact the money are very easy, so easy that they can have as much as you want. Presented? And to the question - why do you have them yet in the desired amount, try as a possible answer to reply, according to which you are very lazy to rake your desired amount of money. Notice I do not say anything, I'm just asking you to submit a picture of the world that's slightly different from the one in which you used to live. You tell me what you're working every day from morning till night, and you can not say about yourself that you are lazy, but the money to you at the same time does not go hard. It is much easier to present it to those who really lazy to do anything, there's at least some compliance with this will. But do not get excited dear friends, I know all your arguments as to why some in this life there is money, while others do not, and how it is not fair, so think most of them are those who are deprived of life in the There is nothing surprising. But that's the mental state you while in such a state that you do not have no chance to change their financial condition, the biggest mistake most of those who have little money - that's their idea of money as something that gets hard labor .

I have dealt with people mainly from this understanding, there is certainly a lot of other situations and stereotypes seated in the minds of people not having money, but it is basic. Money is not given to labor, and to make them not to work, at least physically, we have to work his head while in a particular direction. Money is my friend just created so that one did not work and lived by those who plow from day to day, like damn, trying to earn a living. Remember Ostap Bender of the 12 seats, here are these people, and for such people invented money. Money can not buy happiness, money is not important, and similar statements, specifically formulated for those who have no money, really fundamentally wrong set. The issue of money does not have to be, so it's - well, that the reasoning with respect to water, food, air, shelter, clothing and so on.

Money - it is most necessary, just to be, we're not talking about the food, if we are satisfied, we do not attach importance to the air, as we have it in abundance, and our mental state in this regard, it is peaceful. Can you imagine yourself in, say, a sunken ship, where air supply is limited, how do you think your view of the world will be different from what it usually is? So with the money that we did not value them above what they actually are, and have always had them in the required amount, we need to treat them like to attribute the natural life, which just has to be it. Do not exalt the money to the sky, and getting them into something heroic, just make sure that the money you were going in the desired amount, for example, create a business - this is the best way to earn a lot of money.

50

I understand that in our society, where the worship of the golden
calf, it is difficult to do, but you think so at least a few minutes a
day, preferably before bedtime. Do not ask technical questions,
you first of all it is important to properly configure your psyche,
and only then you will understand how and what to do. If you
have the money became more you raised the salary or you
suddenly get rich, do not think of it as a miracle, take it for
granted, as the law is not only for you but for everyone. This is a
pattern that the air is at all, but not everyone understands this.
That is why we attach great importance, it becomes a problem
for us, it is like a beautiful girl, which all pay attention and she
builds himself a costly madam. But it is necessary to deprive her
attention, even stop to notice it and give it at least some value,
and no matter how beautiful she was, her confidence, and with it
the price will fall through the floor. So the price of a beautiful
woman, as well as a handsome man, is determined not by their
appearance, and attention to them by others, to conclude from
this. Now spend the analogy with money, an inanimate object
with one hand, and their psychological state to another. What
you attach such importance, is a problem for you, is not it, it's
the same for you unattainable girl, inaccessibility that you have
defined for themselves. The man with the money, the same can
be different to look at their lives and the role of money in it,
everything here determines how he earned it and how they came
to him.

51

If this was the result of some mental combinations that
result in money was as I call it invented, the attitude towards them at
such person simplistic and condescending, he did not betray them not to
value and not squandering them, simply because of not wanting to make
them easy prey for others.

And another thing, if the money came from labor, or through a long and
painstaking work, which could not be as heavy and cumbersome as
intense, there is quite a different attitude. You decide how you will make
money, whether you focus on your head, and benefit from the process of
inventing money pleasure that will breathe the air in the open field, or to
bend his back, and drive themselves in the same wreck where this a vital
element is limited. Mental status and not technical issues - that is
important, not only for the money, for all the money only as an example
of how to relate to all this life, where all the problems are only in our
heads.

Chapter 8

«Why do we not want to spend money on yourself ?»

That seems to be, and the money is there, and I want so much - to update your wardrobe, change her hair, take a course of the massage, go to the holiday home.

But there are some more important things, more urgent purchases - and once again we move ourselves into the background, urging that they say, her husband now we need a new computer, or a fashionable men's shoes, and the repair time to make, and children at the sea send. Why is this happening? What really prevents us from taking care of yourself? The failure to spend money on themselves - it is a superficial manifestation of deeper problems. We ask the question differently: why do we care enough about yourself?

This may be due to the breach of maternal care in the first months of life (tired mother did not respond to the cry of a baby, is not always supported him emotionally, and the child does not feel safe). As adults, at some difficult moment, we too can throw your inner child "forget" to go to the doctor, Zayed problem of harmful food, lit ...

Such a mentality is peculiar to communities through difficult times. When enough material resources and survival requires a lot of time and effort to maintain the existence of the collective is more important than the individual ("If you survive all around, and I will survive").

Until now, the country's poorest families and live more united than thriving. Unconscious feeling that "I need less than others", passed down from generation to generation, becoming part of the world order. A decrease in this trend shows the growth of well-being in society. " Changes in the appearance or way of life surely will change something in our lives and our world view. A change, even positive, many are afraid. In my case (quite hard because I spend the money her husband has always been ashamed, even when I was not working forced sitting with a small child) a problem stretches from family units.

Spending money on salons, manicure, beautiful trinkets among our relatives was considered a sign of a frivolous girl, windy lazy girl. The few relatives that currently is allowed, discussed and condemned. As a child, listening to these tough conversations, I absorbed it into itself, so to speak, to the bone.

The result, alas, we have to observe to this day. However, I tell you, it is treated. Long, hard, but treated. And treated nice! We need to sit down and make a list of everything you would want for yourself, your favorite, buy and do. Beat all the goodies on the scale (once a day, once a week, month, year)
Take your organizer and plan all these things and shopping. When all is painted on paper, as well as a good work in advance allocated money from the family budget - will be much less reason to worry Make it a rule to issue a "prize" for every serious or unpleasant task. Before spring cleaning in advance to think of something to thank you. Make an appointment with a hairdresser. Baby new thing. Study your family budget and think about how much money a month without remorse you're willing to spend on themselves and set up a separate expense item with your name. Do not be shy. I've somehow looked at the article "delicious candy" in their home accounting and quiet experience pleasure. And then he went and cut the budget "vkusnyashek" and some other articles of the half. Certainly, in their favor.
And the main thing. Often we look at ourselves in the mirror and smile lovingly and gently sentence the "you're my good girl, you're my beauty, I love you so much!" We are all in the pursuit of happiness: someone a lifetime looking for love, someone is trying to achieve fame, others dream to move to another country. However, no matter what goals we pursue no, most of us have a very simple and clear indicator of happiness - money.

.

The problem is that for many people, this resource is exhausted while our needs and desires only grow and grow. Manufacturers same goods and services, knowing that our weakness throws up new ideas for all purchases, which should certainly make us happy. This is an essential characteristic of the modern world.

"Do you buy things that would experience the fun?"

It is unlikely to ever be able to break this vicious circle of endless consumption, but try to at least temporarily get out of it and look at it from the side it is under our power. Especially because these have long been engaged in science. As you know, there is a dominant method of investing money, which is used by most of the people instead of spending money on a single vivid experience (concerts, exhibitions, folly), we prefer to invest in things that will last longer and it seems to us, endlessly to please us. One of the enemies of happiness is addictive. We buy things to feel happy, and for a while, we experience this feeling. But not for long. New things we capture for a short period, and then we adapt to them. Instead of buying the latest smartphone or a new car, I suggest getting a portion of happiness, spending money on new experiences: go to the exhibition, visit the interesting event, spend time outdoors, develop new skills or risk a parachute jump. Continued growth in absolute income does not increase the level of life satisfaction.

56

For example, to find out how adaptation affects happiness, consider how happy you make material purchases and investment in getting new experiences. Most likely their original investment in the joy of things and the experience was about the same, but over time, the satisfaction of bought items started to decline, while the enjoyment of impressions for which they spent the money, began to grow.

Are short-term experience can make us happier than the long-coveted possession of a physical object? However, oddly enough, the fact that a material thing is always at hand, works against it because we get used to this stuff, and it is gradually becoming the norm, something ordinary for us. But while the joy of the acquisition of material wealth eroding, feelings rooted in our minds and become part of our identity.

"Shopping and rich experiences"

In contrast to the wealth of our experience and our impressions are part of us. You may be very like your stuff, you might even think that part of your personality is somehow connected with certain things, but, nevertheless, they are separated from you. In contrast, your experiences are actually a part of you.

People have not really fond memories, they are quite positive about what happened when it is possible to talk about it.

Some scary and stressful events that happened to us in the past, eventually reinterpreted by us as an invaluable experience, and sometimes even turn into stories that can be told with a smile to a friend

If that you are not convinced to spend money on experiences, here's another good reason: we are less inclined to compare their experience with the impressions of others, while in the sphere of material we often sin that compare, compare, compare (his car neighbor with a car, a telephone with a telephone colleagues, my friends apartment to apartment, etc.).

Wealth is much simpler and easier to compare, that's why we are doing this (how much more expensive your ring? How fast your laptop?).

58

"Intuitive actions"

Of course, we often intuitively feel it all, when there is a
situation of "either - or". Another thing is that sometimes we take
to be the weakness of the desire to renounce all material
calculations and afford to give up on another continent, or to
enroll in the school of Argentine dance rather than to buy
something important, and useful life for our apartments. But as
you see, is not weakness, and our intuition, which knows best
what is good for us and what is bad.

Chapter 9

«Greed people»

Usually greedy people considered to be rich, while the really poor people are much greedier. The rich man is not greedy, it is prudent and economical, in most cases, poor as wasteful and extravagant in their spending, poor people tend to spend more than they earn, often find themselves in debt. According to his observations, I often noticed the difference between the rich and the poor, and I can say with certainty that the poor people more greedy, greedy people terribly. The reason is primarily a social repression as they feel inferior, left out lesser beings compared to others. Usually rich people cause their hatred and anger, jealousy and strong. Therefore, as soon as such a person an opportunity to get a little more, he believes it is a chance for himself and tries to grab everything that is possible.

In such human behavior have always played and are playing in order to use it to their advantage.

The method of lure for people working perfectly without the material goods that others have, have not prepared for much that they would take hold. And it is useless to explain to him that much of what he does not, it is totally unnecessary. The poor man always thinks that he needs something, because it is not. Create equal society yet no one has succeeded, in my opinion it is a utopia, at least as long as the education of the person will not take place in a more equal footing. Not yet prerequisites to the fact that people would have had the same steady psyche and without it there will always be suppressed moral people. Materialism became for them the sole purpose in life to which they aspire, and this materialism, no more than an idea.

This idea can be anything, such as belief in God, or the idea to build a special society with equal rights. Materialism prevails in our world only because it is close to the demand, and although the majority of the needs of the people imposed, all the money and material benefits for the rest of their closest. Although the case as I have already said, is not about money, it's only people who either take you or not, and if society has a negative attitude towards the poor people, strongly oppressing them, the desire to be the same as all, and even better, a poor man It will be manifested in greed. In fact, to meet all their needs, people do not so much need, but know it is only those who have a necessary amount of life.

Or rather, they do not know and understand this, the rest who do not have, do not even know that they will not be enough for as long as they have not received.

If people went hungry as a child, then with high probability it will be obese or too kind to the food. If the person did not have a child clothes, and he had to continue wearing for someone old and tattered clothes, the more likely it will become obsessed with buying their clothes.

All this is so obvious, that it became an iron rule, but not for those who suffer from it. Although there are exceptions, they are familiar to me. There just have to pull out all the subconscious fears and transfer them to the conscious level. Then people will realize that what was already gone, and before him a completely different life in which there is no need to stock all of which he did not have before. Two pants do not wear, do not eat five meals, in three cars just did not go, so why all this is necessary? Greed, originating because of fear of losing everything and the fear of something I do not have time. That's only in this fear and its corresponding behavior, the person loses most importantly, their lives.

All my life for something to chase, to the grave, it is not life, and if f you've been born into a poor family, use it as a stimulus to the desire to live in dignity, but do not be greedy to the smallest detail. Greed never helped, she always comes up with the stupidity and madness, poisoning life and sometimes ruining it.

Chapter 10

«What is your wealth?»

Many of my friends often ask me what is the wealth of the person. And still much to discuss on this topic. Just the fact that a clear answer to this question. Everyone must determine for himself what is for him the wealth. I will give some definitions and considerations that will help answer the question, what is a person's wealth. Mostly controversial definition of "wealth." Many sources said that "the richness - an abundance of a man tangible and intangible assets, such as money, capital goods, real estate or personal property." But what is the abundance? It is a relative concept. In one country, one car per family - have an abundance, but in another country for more than two cars per family - is the norm. "By the wealth, it can also include access to health care, education and culture." But this definition in all the rich people of North Korea, although with an abundance of "tangible and intangible assets" in the first definition of the problem in humans.

In sociology, the rich man is the one who has a significant value in relation to other members of society.

Here I began to understand, but I have a question - how to determine the boundaries of society? The world is becoming more open and closed societies disappear. The richest one Somali village is one of the poorest people on the plane bound for London. In economics, wealth is defined as the difference between assets and liabilities at a given time. But it usually is not determined by the wealth of the person, and its capital, although the difference is not so great. And for example, in the biblical sense - a way of life in which revenues exceed expenses. It is the truth too. Finally, "The opposite of wealth is poverty." This is rightly so.

All wealthy people know what is for their wealth and willing to give his definition of this concept. But their definition - different. For example, I have a friend who says that he will be rich when he can live on the interest from interest. Think about it! He wants to live in the capital, and not even on the interest from his capital and the interest on the interest from his capital. This friend of mine knows how much it receives interest on interest practically every hour. When we go to dinner, he knows how much is dinner and how much he has earned interest on interest, while we dined.

If he earned during dinner more than eaten, he is happy. I'm here as a calculated and found that if he spends on dinner $ 100 an hour, its capital should be no less than the US $ 86,400,000 and generate at least 10% per annum - that's what a man's wealth for my rich friend.

Most likely, such a definition of wealth a man like my friend, for you are not fit. Most likely, your own definition of wealth is much more modest. And that's fine. You can define wealth as some figure number of capital or number of monthly income. For example, you can define that for you wealth - millions of dollars of capital in the form of deposits, shares, real estate, which brings you an annual income of $ 50 000. Just remember that a million dollars now - a relatively small amount. Many houses in the center of New York worth more than a million dollars and many machines are more expensive than you can get a million dollars in interest over the year. So first determine for yourself your goals in life where you want to live, how much you want to spend - for a year, and 5 for 20-30 years ahead, and then to determine for themselves what is wealth. If you want to retire in 60 years, to move to a house on the beach in Spain and send children to study at Harvard, then you need to determine exactly what the riches you need in order to fund all of these your plans. What is it? And where to store this wealth - in the bank in shares in real estate? More precisely, unambiguously, all suitable answer to this question is no. But the idea is that you are at least roughly defined what wealth for you personally. After all, if you do not specify the target, you can not achieve it.

For me, the wealth - is to have enough money to not have to worry about their absence in the present and in the future.

65

How much it? I do not have a specific amount. I'm not worried about the money now because my income a little higher than my expenses.

In principle, I am worried about the money in the future, because I'm still young and do not know what country I will live in the future, how great is my family, what will be our burden. But I'm doing everything to ensure that when this future will come gradually, I had enough money to fund it.

Chapter 11

«Successful and unsuccessful people»

Success or failure in our lives, this is not the whims of fate, which is supposedly for us to decide who will succeed and who will bypass a success, but only the result of our own activities and, above all, is the result of our conscious or unconscious choice. By nature, people are the same, however, as a result of the choices each of us makes some people rise up while others are at the bottom, and even sink to the bottom.

Success and failure are quite an understandable pattern, and thus, successful and unsuccessful people are formed quite an understandable way. Given the fact that we are all cut from the same cloth, even being at the bottom, none of us have no reason to feel inferior to those whose lives admiration and envy.

After all, in fact, successful and unsuccessful people is the same people by nature, but while choosing different ways of life living in different life laws, adhering to different ideologies, to think differently, and in connection with this action on different logical algorithms. To help you better understand my point, I suggest you, dear readers, to ask ourselves the question of what distinguishes a successful person from the loser, in your view, and what distinguishes you from the person of a successful person, you feel successful?

Try not to be biased and not look for excuses to himself or others, just pay attention to the facts that are taking place in your life and the lives of others. Personally, I can discern one very negative qualities are inherent in every human being with whom one know how to fight, but unfortunately, there is no other, and, as a result, become a victim of this quality. This my friends too lazy, can not say with certainty what nature has bestowed us with you this quality, but it is an integral part of each of us that we probably have to hold on a short leash, otherwise it would have completely overcome. The man successful in life - this is the first man made the right choice, and as such can only be the choice of the active life, and secondly a man who does that is it at work, it is not a passive person who waits for luck herself fall on his head.

I could list you a lot of useful qualities of successful on a person's life, a man who obtained everything that he had planned and what it does, but this without my written many books, so I will not repeat the widely known the truth, at least in their familiar form. On them, you will read elsewhere. In principle, any successful person book, replete with all these important human qualities, which you need to know, and the main thing that you need to develop in themselves.

Therefore, to give you something new in this sense, I suggest you think that's more of what the fact - a successful man - a man who turns his plans. Do not neglect friends my request to reflect on their own about it, of course, I'll give you all the answers in this article that I want to give, but it's still time you read an article on psychology, you should understand all of what I have here said, because only this will allow you realize my words and reconfigure to another wave. Otherwise, it will be like my meal you prepared hot cakes, that you may be pleased to tuck into, but baking them you do not learn.

And so, if you have already thought of a successful person is over the person who gets what he's up to, then you will not surprise my statement that each person in this life is successful, the result is for everyone. The result - a finished product of your activities, and she, in turn, was made possible by your choice and what you do for yourself conceived. You know what I mean, no losers in this life, there is no unsuccessful people from the logical point of view, there are only people who do not have what others have, and that they themselves would like to have. That's just we do all different things, some are doing things closest to what they want, others are doing the same things similar to what they want, but what they do not realize, and it is a question of the wrong choice.

That's why I've always said and I say that for example people do not really want money, if after work, he was lying on the couch and watching TV, when a day off is to drink beer with friends or entertain any other way, the money he did not need, that he was not saying. Here grow a wineskin lounging on the couch and sipping a beer can, and a choice of such a man, it was his idea to reality, and can in no doubt that he will succeed. Raising awareness, that's what will help each of us to become the most successful is the concept, to whom we are accustomed to calling it because to know that you really have to, then do it. The rest of the brakes are not essential, it will not work if I can not, to hell with all this chaff, if you decided on the fact that you need from life - just go and do. Being a good psychologist, I proved during all the years of his work in the meantime I did not know how to write and to present in writing all your thoughts. And if you read my first article including this site, you can grab his head, why I never do that. But being a dog, all-knowing but not knowing how to explain it through writing, I did, as you see, write and let me still have not learned to do it properly, I will not stop.

You understand that the main thing here, the main thing here is just to do what you think is right, and the result will be, in any case, a different matter as it will be, but I do in any case, are satisfied. Who paid basis I have consulted fourteen people from time to time the question comes up for a free consultation, and after all only a year ago, I created a website, and with his own hands, but I can pay for it.

This way is very important to be able to do everything with their own hands, at least of what to do with your life very closely, because it points to your ability, but rather in their immensity. Tell me, friend, can I call his work a success, and that's so unusual, which can each of you? There is nothing unusual here, there is no secret of success that all so ardently seek, or you do everything necessary to achieve the desired you, or you're doing something else, what success is guaranteed. Maybe some of you will rely on the ignorance of what they should do, what I often hear the nature of their activities.

What this saying refers to ignorance is not the type of activity, which should be dealt with, and ignorance of their own desires, which people do not really decided. Do not you know a lot, we are something we do not know, and apparently will never know. But what prevents you know what prevents you from taking a step in the direction of their own desires, if you and he decided, only lazy, what else could it be? A lot of people complain about their fate, they find their lives unhappy and are waiting that someday things will change for the better, that at the behest of external forces, there will be something that will be for them the good, the truth is that it must be a miracle is , no one really can not say, all just platitudes say, pointing to the perpetrators on both sides.

If I offered assistance to such people, they would have said what and how they should do, and then their life is guaranteed to improve, they will not listen to me and will not do anything. Although that means if I did it many times and still do, but very few people need the help of this kind, few want to become a successful and happy person, this is the whole point.

Well, if a person does not want to, if it is more comfortable with another life if he wants another really force him to do something against his will, as it is not very reasonable for a reasonable person. Let's not talk about others, let's talk about you, dear reader, I believe that I speak to each of you personally. You have already understood, that successful and unsuccessful people - it is the same people who just want a different life, no more differences in people, not even too lazy alike are at all, but some are too lazy to be by anyone while others are too lazy to be people. What do you want from life you personally, and what's stopping you get it? Something you do not know, right? You do not know how you do the right thing to do, where to start? You have read these lines this article of mine, well, then, the person you're not lazy, anyway, to read you can not be lazy, which means you are ready to work, ready to do something, rather than waiting until all by itself happens. Remarkably, this is the most important thing, I hope the desires with their, you have already decided, because, at this stage, the creative work of your brain is finished. The following is a physical process of implementing their plans for you, impeccably disciplined and doing that, you get everything you want.

Place the creativity in your life has to be, it is not only the dream of something good, it is also many variations of your actions, of which the singularity depends on what you consider yourself to success. You see at the top of the page the word "consultation fee" - you know what it is - this is what you need when you do not know. Payments that will give you the opportunity to change your life, it is the most profitable investment that can only be because you are investing in its perfection, this applies to all the moments when you pay for knowledge. In such an investment can not be the price, because it is priceless, but the price can be the set man who pays his personal time with you, and at the time, too, agrees that the price is not small. So what issues to take advantage of my helping hand, which is stretched to you, for what you are willing to pay money and to whom you are willing to pay them. Are you happy to pay the alcohol and tobacco industry, you pay the garment factory, cellular companies, automakers, who you have to pay for that?

And what you get in return, temporary pleasure, see how thruput and shake out your money above industry, or rather, their cream while your's life goes on, it does not change for the better, you do not even come close to the life which people live, which you pay for that many, perhaps you consider a successful life. Well, what you do, do not you deserve to pay themselves, so as not to spend money on an infinite satisfaction of their desires and be content with little in this life.

Why not pay yourself and do not invest in their own, and not someone else's future? You say that buying a paid service from me, you pay me, yes, you pay me, I work, I do not sell you the air, of course, it is worth the money you pay them to me.

But the money may be gone forever and can come back several times increase, this friend called and investment, and to pay me, so that's paying me, you essentially pay for themselves, for I have given you a lot more than getting from you. And it is more than I pay in terms of money, but if you judge a moral pleasure I get the opportunity to change the lives of a single person, but together and change the world for the better, then it is very expensive. Personally, I do my work gives meaning to live, and with the money I have problems as such no longer exist, it does not believe the most difficult task in life. So think over how you want to be successful and believe that success for yourself, because if you do something that does not fit with your desire, hence a desire false. Do not want to gain knowledge from me, learn from my system does not want to deal with me, do not trust me, do not like my methods, my position in life, he does not like me? Well, I'm an adult, will not be offended, but you get the other person from whom you will learn everything that interests you. People who know that you need a lot, and if you want, you will find them all. And if you can call it the secret of success, how many would have liked, well, let it be a secret, but by and large, how can it be a secret so obvious, it's a secret only to those who are too lazy to look at the facts and to understand everything.

Chapter 12

«What is most valuable to you?»

The most valuable thing a man can have - that is what is in his mind, not matter how physically strong you are or what your social status is important, how smart you are. At the same time, when we are talking about the mental abilities of a person, we often mean everything that is mainly due to its memory. Now, if people read a lot, and many remember from your reading, and, more accurately, the better, it is often perceived as a high rate of his mental faculties, while the understanding they read and about the ability to use what has been learned, it comes much less. That's why people often vote for these politicians, this is an example of that much to say, to speak beautifully, but it is doing nothing, or doing, but it was something other than what they said. We must understand that knowledge, we are pretty smart and clever, even facial expressions, which, as you know, is the most stupid things in this world, it's not a sign of intelligence.

We have to be practical, efficient and deliberate in their actions, our thinking should be critical, pragmatic, flexible. Here then, we can consider ourselves smart, regardless of the amount of knowledge that we possess. Our brain with you - it is a powerful computer that is capable of doing just incredible calculations, which needless to say are designed to meet our needs, both primary and secondary. You may be weak physically, can take a very low position in the social hierarchy, and even rejection by society but your fate will depend not on it, and from your mental abilities. There is nothing more important in the life of your mental abilities, you must first invest their energy, time, money, it is the most profitable investment, which only can be. All that you have now, that's all you can be lost, no matter what are the reasons for the fact, you can take away everything you have in the material sense, or if it comes to people, they can leave you, or betray. But your mind, your head, you take much more difficult, of course, and it can happen, but this is the will of the case. But as life, to worry it does not happen if you keep your sanity, you can always recover all lost and more. They say the most terrible punishment of God - this is when it deprives a person of reason, partly because, except that I think that the worse is not it worse to be common sense, but to be lazy and do not develop their mental abilities, not to develop its most important organ which It makes us stronger.

The man lost his mind, nothing to regret, does not understand and is mediocre at which it can be quite comfortable even at the last stage of decomposition of the degradation.

76

When you understand what you need to do and not to do, this is much more difficult, it's like when anesthesia awareness when you are feeling, and do nothing can not lack the will, it is the same paralysis of your brain as paralysis during anesthesia. But among the majority of people who are under anesthesia, your mental faculties, who knows what makes him stronger, but does nothing for their own development. Many of the most valuable of their body is in suspended animation, they do not use it, preferring to act instinctively and on a pre-rooted patterns. A typical misconception is taking place in relation to the money that we have with them is most important, their presence, or enough of them?

No friends, no money is important and not the number, or even create asset cash flows, it is important to the ability to create these streams, it is important to understand how things work, in the case of need to build everything that you need. Once again - in this life you can lose everything you have on the melon moment, everything can disappear, but most importantly do not lose your head, its banks above all, give it all if needed, and leave the head. After the gray matter that is in your head is capable of such miracles, and you can not imagine, can not, most likely in relation to itself, but, in fact, examples of human possibilities we all see.

And now think even that's something to - that each of you have friends that any other human brain is wired the same way, and with it your only recourse may be different from those of other people's actions, which may be more or less successful than you.

Knowing how the soup is cooked, you can cook it constantly, and learn this once, then only need to use their knowledge when needed. People, money, power, a sense of all this phenomenon is not permanent, everything is subject to change, and the main goal of any reasonable person should not be these pseudo-values, and the desire to be the smartest way possible. Look at the people who govern mankind, though not all of them you can see, but some do not hide their faces, you feel how the mental ability of these people is superior to yours? It does not even need to see, namely to feel the force because she has always felt an instinct primarily, and only then we realized if we are making efforts to realize it. Only here you have in any case should not worry about it, because as I said, you have the same authority valuable as any other person in this world.

Again, I repeat, it does not matter who you are, what you are and where you are, no matter where you were born, no matter what you have, and it does not matter, a member of society you are, you have at your disposal the gray matter in his head, and can his help everything. I am always amazed cases of suicide as a very gifted people, is completely healthy and capable of many things, committed suicide because of temporary mental health problems when their calculations regarding the prospects of their future - came to a standstill.

After all, that there did not happen in the life of a suicide, the most important thing remains with him, otherwise, they would not have dared to take such a step, but the main body is unfortunately made a miscalculation in relation to himself, and, as a result, decided to self-destruct. I know that if I can convey to each of you dear readers, understanding how your brain is important to you, and your mental abilities may develop at your desire is boundless, you will never be one of those who commit such a senseless and unnatural acts like suicide.

Moreover, you have about yourself and cease to feel at least some discomfort, because all that is in your life is the result of your mental abilities are developing, you can accordingly change their lives, and even the lives of others. And returning to the powers that be, it is worth noting them a clear understanding of what I write here, it's not my reasoning, and even surveillance is primarily a result of communication with these people, and then to conclusions and conscious patterns.

Do not run like a squirrel in a wheel to it, that in itself does not exist for those illusions of false values, with which you deliberately confusing, and you react so easily. I know these people very much, I did not immediately come to an understanding of the values that are truly valuable and which we can live the life of the winners, and not to be exploited mediocrity.

Of course, not only your mind is your strength, you have to take care of the health of your body is your vehicle and it should be working, and your brain is the tool without which survive in this life is very difficult. People who do not give their mental abilities of a large value of life as such do not, it's just a meaningless existence, dependent on external factors. Well-developed mental abilities, and have a positive impact on the human psyche, which is no place for panic, there is no place to stress, there are no meaningless emotional displays. Do not forget that it is thanks to people more advanced mental abilities, he rose above the rest of the animal world, in which many of his views are much stronger physically. One more thing I want to tell friends - this is very important, life teaches us all the time, everywhere and always, it gives us a very important life lessons that direction again, the fact that we were becoming stronger. But their assimilation depends on our intelligence, so at least, his intellectual development, life becomes more simple and understandable because you notice the numerous tips and are evidence that there is this life throws us. And when you see, you know, and all can be calculated, can you be in such a case, the problems associated with the unpredictable situations that you could not predict, prepare for, respectively, or even prevent their occurrence? The answer I think, is obvious to you, therefore, appreciate the most valuable, develop their mental abilities, and finally, get out of this terrible ana bio nogo state in which perhaps some of you, is your brain. Do not let others think for you, think for yourself, other people should only serve as a source of information for you, but it means chewing.

Chapter 13

«Rich and Poor» principle of thinking.

Rich people are learning life. But it is not only the traditional study at the institute, and a visit to various courses, workshops, seminars, reading, teaching literature, specialized viewing sites, video courses, that is, self-education.Poor people are sure to start in life give them education received in school, secondary technical and higher, higher is better.

What is important for them to study at the institute, and it will better the education the better they will be able to arrange his life. After graduation, the learning process for the majority of poor people ever ends.

Rich and poor people relate differently to the selection of works. The principle of the rich people in the choice of the method of earnings is that they choose the work that they like, which they have dreamed since childhood, they get sick.

But most importantly, they prefer to work for themselves rather than on someone, even if their career starts against the employment of a foreign company, it is only in order to earn the starting capital to open a business. Rich people do not keep all the forces for their work, if it is something they are not satisfied, they are not afraid to change it, and are constantly in search of new perspectives. In general, work on his uncle for successful people is the way to nowhere.

For poor people the main criteria in the selection of the work are its compliance with their specialty and a number of wages (and not only official but also the so-called left-wing money). The main course was the size of earnings. Having found such a place of work, they will hold on to it with all his strength, in every possible way to fawn before the authorities, and even go to vileness in respect of their colleagues to eliminate competitors in this lucrative post

Incomes

Thinking rich and poor people in terms of earnings also differs radically. Rich people always focused on passive income. They understand that their time and energy are not unlimited, unlike money, which can become more and more. Wealthy people use their time and effort not to make at the moment, but in order to create a kind of asset that will bring them a passive income even when they stop working on it, or whether their work would be less intense. At the same successful people tend to create themselves as much as possible different sources of passive

income: they open a business, invest in real estate, buying
securities, etc., that is, increase your wealth their assets, income.
At the same time, they are willing to take risks.

For poor people, the main source of income is active income.
Moreover, most often only one source for the salary. They work
hard to earn more money at one time: get a premium on the
results of the month. Once they are for some reason no longer
work in their personal budget revenues as well stop. Among all
investment options are poor people prefer to bank deposits
because they are clear and reliable. But that is not all: many of
them just keep their money under the pillow

Lifestyle

The habits of rich people sure to include healthy lifestyle,
exercise, active recreational activities. They are at least 3-4 times
a week to the gym, do many daily morning jog and workout.
Rest rich people prefer the outdoors, in the ecologically clean
places. Many of them like extreme entertainment: rock climbing,
scuba diving, etc. Despite the busy schedule, they can always
identify at this time.

Poor people are, for the most part, involved in sports and try to
keep yourself in shape only in adolescence. Next, entering into
adulthood, beginning to work, they begin to believe that this is
not to come home from work tired and flop on the couch.

The evening watching TV is what is their vacation. But when it comes to a large-scale holiday it soon produced noisy celebrations and gatherings at the restaurant with plenty of food and drink. We can also imagine sometimes allow a good rest! so talk about it themselves poor and losers. And even if they go on vacation for some tour, the most important in their program are just such events.

Food

Rich and poor people even eat differently (and not so much in terms of the cost of food consumed, but in terms of the approach to food). Rich and successful people eat only high-quality and healthy products. And, importantly, they never overeat, eat in moderation and in time (often literally on schedule).

Poor people often do not think about your diet in general, they eat what is available to them, what they can afford, and if there is a possibility. And, interestingly, actually afford them, and the most useful products: vegetables, fruits, poultry, eggs, cereals, etc., but they are choosing is harmful: sausage, pork, flour products. Maybe it will seem paradoxical, but poor people often eat too much, which leads to excess weight and health problems. Well, the holidays are generally gorge so that then can not move!

Receiving the information

The principles of rich people are to receive information from trusted and reliable sources. After all, they are well aware that who owns the information he owns the world and has been actively trying to use this rule to achieve their own goals in their work. Rich people always screen out information trash. They read only useful books that carry valuable information for self-development, almost do not watch TV, do not read the tabloids, do not visit entertainment sites.

Poor people are accustomed to getting information from television news sites and social networks. Some even hang out there all the time and feel uncomfortable, if for some reason missed the evening news. They like to watch entertaining talk shows, feature films, reading detective stories and soap operas, and then discuss it all with friends and colleagues. Rest of the work is being held in the act.

Circle of friends

Rich and poor people differently from their social circle. The rich tend to maximize it, especially people even richer and more successful than they are. They surround themselves with people who motivate them to self, next to which they are getting better.

Rich and successful people always tend to analyze and learn from their more successful friends. Social circle of poor people makes the same people as they are. And to the rich and successful they are, or envy, or contempt: that's how snickering, are cashing in at our expense! Persuading thereby ourselves that the rich be bad. They are convinced that the rich people live in their own world, in which they will never get there, but because they are not at all interesting.

Attitude to money

We should also highlight the thinking, principles and habits of the rich and the poor in relation to money. Wealthy people see money as a personal capital that is capable of doing for their new money. The principle of a rich man is this: The more I will have the money, the more I earn! When it comes to regular cash flows, it is, first of all, think about where to invest the money so that they brought the most revenue at the lowest risk. This truly rich people are a fairly modest lifestyle and never show off their wealth. Poor people see money as a tool for life, they earn money to spend. The principle of a poor man's next: The more I will have the money, the more I can afford to buy!

After receiving the money, he thinks only about what is best to spend it. As soon as the poor man starts to earn a little more than those around him, he immediately tries in every way to show it to others: buy expensive clothes and accessories, spending money on expensive entertainment, sent to the foreign resort, change the cell phone, the car begins to take a taxi.

86

Goals and planning

Rich and successful people have always set themselves targets, and, as a global, life and short-term: a year, a month or even a day. Moreover, the purpose of these tend to be very ambitious and, at first sight, unreachable, they are fixed on paper, their performance is constantly reviewed, if necessary, adjust the targets are exposed. In addition, the habits of rich people are part-time planning, implementation of specific measures to achieve these goals. They are always diary or organizer. Their working day is often painted a scarce resource, they perform many diverse tasks and at the same time to all.

Poor people often also think that set themselves the goal, but in fact, it is not goals and dreams. Because they never fixed, and to reach them not to take any action. Often these goals simply state the most ordinary, vitally necessary things: to buy an apartment, make repairs, to educate a child. Either dream are abstract in the spirit I want to have a million dollars.
Poor people do not plan their time, their work, their finances, they are always somewhere in a hurry, and still did not have time. For them, planning a waste of time, and so is not enough.

Fate

And finally, the rich and the poor completely different attitudes to their
way of life. The most important principle of rich people is this: they are
sure to make their own destiny. They focus on what depends on them
that they themselves can do to change your life for the better. The
reasons for all their victories and defeats, they are looking for, first of
all, in itself, analyzed their experience, learn from mistakes, make
conclusions. Poor people are always waiting for the favors of destiny.
And to be precise, supportive influence of some external factors beyond
their control: when they raise wages and pensions, create jobs, make
affordable prices, etc. In their failures, in their poverty, they always
blame the outside world: the state, the government, the oligarchs, the
bosses, and sometimes even friends and relatives, but, of course, but not
himself. What is not intended to change the destiny, that's their life
principle. So live rich and poor. Here they are principles of life and
habits, thinking of the rich and the poor. As you can see, they are
different in everything.

And it once again explains why the rich get richer and the poor get
poorer! Because they just think and develop in completely different
directions.

Chapter 14

«Build grandiose plans»

The fact that each of us will do in this life depends on what each of us plans to put in front of him. The more ambitious your plans, the more they resemble the plans of a madman, the more chances you have to jump over your head. I have often noticed that people actually have as much as they would like to have. All this is expressed primarily in our dreams that we mistakenly share in the dream is real and fantasy. Once a person hears the word impossible, and starts to believe in it, it immediately in my head there is an obstacle that actually makes it impossible to venture. Nothing is impossible, but for some reason we do not think so, apparently thinking patterns ingrained in our minds. Unfortunately, in one degree or another, all of us suffer from it may have to be crazy to do the impossible.

By myself, I can say that even the possibility of realizing any of its undertakings, I often doubt the possibility of its implementation.

Swipe your thinking, should be like the expanding universe, you have to understand that what you think the limit of your ability, you have defined themselves. I will not talk about creative visualization and the materiality of thought, because my work is related primarily to the human psyche, and that is the basis of our mental state, I can conclude that in our mind allows us to pursue our goals. The man who used to be content with little, never get more, he's just not ready for it, he did not wait. You should not be content with little, there's no need, you should always strive for more, and then it's necessary you will always be. Never an athlete will not be the winner if there is to think about how to be at least in the top ten. He is not psychologically ready to win, and thus will not fully lay out, not to mention the self-fulfillment that is hidden in each of us. Also, a person who thinks only about how he would not die of hunger will never become a millionaire, he just does not know how it could all look like. Only the best possible results, the craziest and unreal should be in your head, just an attempt to reach them, you will be able to awaken all of your power and all your potential. That means pushing the limits of the imagination, which generally should be removed, there is no framework - no restrictions. And when you have nothing to limit, and that does not stop, God knows, you reach some peaks. Want to make a million, think about how to make a hundred million, want to raise one hundred kilograms lift a hundred and fifty. Imagine that one hundred percent, this is not the limit, and spread to a hundred and ten, and even more if necessary.

90

And most importantly, believe in their own, even the craziest ideas, do not doubt, because you can doubt in anyone else, but not in itself, in fact, you love and respect yourself, except you, no one of you does not care. Give yourself a promise to give the word to do everything possible to realize his dream into reality, even the most ambitious plan, you will become a reality if keep your word to yourself. Any promise can be broken, except the promises given to me, because promise yourself, believe in yourself, and challenge any scale, you will be on the shoulder. Think as much as possible on a large scale, never themselves do not limit, do not believe in the fact that something is impossible, and does not violate the words of himself, believe in yourself and all you get.

Chapter 15

«Any change is always for the better!»

If we talk about change, I always remember my first job and the first girl who put it mildly were not very. And first and second were my mistakes, in a series of my youth, inexperience and stupidity, because of which I have little life kicked. And then it seemed to me that all this is what I need, it is this work and that the woman should be in my life, and it is necessary to think that I am much grieved lost both. However, the old and the good law keeps talking to us about the fact that all the changes are always for the better, as always worked flawlessly and I ended up doing what I'm doing now, I have a wonderful family. But if then, in time, would not have happened did, I would not have come to such a life, which is now fully satisfied if the people I had known would not have delivered me and everything would be going on, as usual, I would not have grown .

92

With such a lyrical note, I started not by chance, I often cite the example of his life, when I communicate with people who are experiencing difficult times in their lives. In this world, which has never been and will not be stable, can happen anything: you can be fired or you go broke, you throw a loved one, or you fell out with your friends, so anything can happen, and then you will feel that everything life has stopped. And that seems to be wrong, damn wrong, believe me. I understand what's going on in the soul of a man whose life is undergoing significant change, they are a revolution, changing everything at once.

And I know it's not like a psychologist who sees people's feelings, but as a person who experienced in his life the same time, so I started with, where I began. All life is in the dynamics of this process, life itself is a process, and the process, in turn, defines such a thing as life. You can not live in constant conditions, is not life, it is a miserable likeness. And because if your life change happens, it is only because you have not created them ourselves, seeing our Almighty toromznutost, he changes our living conditions, you can understand so. And any change, without exception, are opening up new opportunities, they make you rethink your life, to understand what prospects you have to realize their dreams.

Anchor in life you do not need, you need a speaker.

Perhaps certainly something should not occur as a revolutionary, as they say that you lived out of a suitcase, of course values such as family, a loved one, the children should have a constant value for us, it is of course ideal. But if it just so happens that all changed when the change came, and you could not do anything about it, so it should be, you just have to understand the importance of them in his life. Life with the psychological attitude, willing to any changes actually simplify it so much that you're not worried about something, you are in control in their lives that can control, and that goes away from you, you absolutely no worries. If at one time in my life it would change, I would be unlikely to become a businessman, hired work would become my only source of income in life, and next to me would have been quite a decent man, and I is not highly reliable. And that is why I advocate that every person is directed to their lives, and not wait to the will of fate that decides to change to fresh water foul. If you see a dead end in your life, look for themselves a way out, do not be afraid to change your life, what could happen wrong, you go to the light, so we are still going to be there, sooner or later. Actually not so critical, in most cases, nothing in your life you are not in danger, but you're afraid of change because you imposed a sense of stability and peace to which you supposedly have to strive for. At any moment in the life of each of us can expect anything to happen, and we, or rather you're not ready for this, is this normal?

Try to include your imagination and imagine that something happened that you think will never happen with you.

94

It is not so difficult, each of you, this will not only have to be afraid of scary thoughts about what might happen suddenly. You just imagine such a situation and then think that you have done in this case, and whether it was the right decision. Simulate different scenarios in my life, and determines the order of their actions when they occur. The aim is not to podstelit straw wherever possible, and to prepare you psychologically, you can even record the order of their actions on the paper. Because if something goes even what you expect, in principle, your emotions can cloud your mind, and most likely it will be so. Now calm and relatively stable environment, you are a sober man in his right mind understand that some changes in your life arise for a long time, and that they are actually the better, think about it, for sure there is something that for a long time it's time to change. However, as soon as such a situation occurs, in the best case, if you are going to make a decision at the worst if it's all going to happen without you, how will you feel then? And just turning to take root in his mind the plan of action, or read them in their prefabricated records, you will be able to clearly and do not panic, do what they should. Otherwise, emotions can lead you, I know whereof I speak, I felt it myself and saw a lot of people who could not control himself.

95

So what can this article, and will set your mind to apparently correct wave, and you can understand the importance of the ongoing changes in your life, understand that they are always for the better, you get more than they lost, and so on and so forth. But by the change must be prepared, the psychological preparation for them is very important for the soft decision any possible scenario of events in your life. So my friends include the imagination, do not let happiness find you by surprise, you know it comes in a mask and unexpectedly.

Chapter 16

«Overcome anxiety and fear»

We are living with you in troubled times, terrible times, you can not trust anyone, everywhere we in danger and survive in a world very, very hard. Is it really because if the world is cruel and unfair as it seems, and it seem to us at all? If you think in terms of a person who is looking for answers to all the challenges that life presents him, then of course, yes, the world as it is and it seems like it always has something to fear.

But if the only slightly different approach to all of the negative result, to which you come as you gain experience of life, in general, you will see that you did not have to worry and be afraid of you, too, does not cost anything. As it is necessary to approach life, how to take it and not worry about anything? First of all friends, you need to replace their faith in the knowledge and hope for a systematic approach and understand that as it was not turned your life at the helm stand you, and even if the wind today, you do not have the associated tomorrow he can start to blow in your side.

The main thing is not to move away from the wheel, the main thing is always to turn it into the desired direction, then you sail where you want to sail. But I will cover you with platitudes, in the end, I was not the first by whom do you can hear and probably not the last, because you and I have something to do with the fact that he was sitting in our heads, we are not perfect in his worldview. Speaking more specifically, I want to understand a little about a systemic approach to live, which, in principle, deprive you of excitement and a variety of concerns, and in part will save you from fear, which can be a cause of uncertainty in your life. In every problem and every task, there is a solution, and if you stick to a clear algorithm of actions, in principle, decide any problem. It remains only to find that algorithm, and it certainly can be done, you just have to do it, and here it is this lesson, we may contact you to name a systematic approach to their lives.

Pragmatism is another integral part of your successful inner world, but it certainly should be able to build logical chains and greatly expand their horizons of knowledge. If you read a lot of books, clever books, then you will have a broader view of the world, is also extremely important, I would even say it is strategically important - to communicate with intelligent people. And those can be called who my friends lives are called a full life and not philosophize quoting the classics in a communal kitchen. And here we have already come to such a concept as the belief that of course gives people the power, but not as big as the knowledge, believe and know it is very far from each other things.

Faith sometimes helps to cope with the fear, but knowing what to do, understanding the trends and vision of possible results, in principle, make people confident and without fear. You do not have to worry about when you know that sail to the ground, and not just believe it. If a believer for any reason shaken his faith, his life loses meaning, so that even if faith was false, people hold on to it as a saving straw as the only hope that faith will help them through difficulties. While as a clear knowledge of what is and can be, and most importantly the knowledge that it is possible to find a solution, not way not confuse a person, but it is a mental state, to which he had come, and how people come to his unblemished faith. You do not have to worry about if you say to watch a movie with a happy ending, which has watched many times and you know that in the end everything will be fine. With this attitude to life, you just will not survive if something will prevent you live, though certainly be a complete master of your life you do not get though much of it can be kept under control. Afraid man can only when you do not know how he would solve the problem that he had that very fear is that any uncertainty bothers us, and anxiety - it's a mild form of fear, after which can be very severe form, up to paranoia. Yes, in fact, the life of modern man is paranoid because people are always afraid of something, feel the excitement almost every day, and this often causes them to hasty action, which could lead to even more disastrous consequences.

What are the real potential threats, each of us can be in life, for example if you and we will consider only those whose probability is average or above average? Certainly not a little, but I think that all the same list is not very long, and the list each of us can work from and to. So you basically can find ready-made solutions to those likely threats that somehow can affect your life negatively, and even if you do not work to prevent them, in any case, you will be able to solve any of these problems. Having the correct sequence of actions even for a limited number of threats, you'll have much less to worry, you will not be afraid of what the media frighten you constantly. Only now, some people manage to be afraid of the threats, the probability of which is negligible, some fear the meteorite that can fall to the ground while others fear the end of the world, others of an alien invasion, and so on. Is not that crazy friends, and, in fact, a lot of such examples, and they all have a negative impact on the psyche of the people clogging their brains completely unnecessary challenges that it is faced with. Of course, our life without surprises will not do, but if a person has developed a habit of looking for the solution of any problems in his life, and most importantly have a craving for it, you will not be surprised as a man, how much interest the. It's hard to overcome all fear of man, as a psychologist, I had to deal with its various manifestations, among those who appealed to me for help, there were people with various life situations. Yes, and I like a lot of people solved their problems by overcoming fear and anxiety, but it is easier to do if you take into service competently and correctly from a logical point of view of the installation.

Human psychology is formed according to the settings which guide and attitudes, in turn, are the product of the social environment in which a person is born, it grows and then lives. While some people live in a constant atmosphere of fear and problems, making them out of all the others live in absolute peace of mind, that part of their life that they control is significant that in this case they fear. Do not believe friends, we must know, do not hope, it is necessary to systematically solve their problems and be pragmatic man, so surprises in your life will be less. And about love, I would say - do not love, it is necessary that you love, then you and this will be no problem. Of course all of this have to be adjusted because it is working with the brain, so your inner state on which to base all your behavior, so we call our psychology. That's why people go to psychologists because it is the same as a specialist electrician or plumber if you do not know how to set themselves properly, contact the person who knows how to do it. Little good psychologist, I'm doing this conclusion because I observe around me a lot of concern and frightened people did not know how to solve their problems, predict the future, and just be aware of what and how to do them better. But if you want, you will find a specialist, just as willing to learn martial arts, he is a true master who could make him a better soldier.

Chapter 16

«Installation of victory»

I'm crazy to hear about how some athletes, giving an interview to the sports, set goals other than the first point at which they are in their own words did not even count. The ability to get into the top ten, or simply perform successfully - that's their goal, from that, I honestly just sick. How and what they and sports commentators, is considered a success and praised the athletes if they have won the second, third, tenth, and so on the place. It is simply impossible to watch, especially me, a man who knows about the internal installation, which shall be guided by the athlete. I am familiar with the people, which in Soviet times were preparing athletes for competition, is a coach and psychologists, some of whom I have learned a lot. What prevents a person to see himself the everywhere winner? Self-doubt - yes, of course, but where does it come from, why do people have to a question, he himself - is the one to whom he has to trust in the first place and whom to believe in spite of no matter what? Yes, everything is very simple, we have too many reasons why we are losers and why someone is better than us.

We know not what we should know and consider it an objective point of view. Talk to a failure with respect to any of his ambitious ideas, and he will give you a million arguments against it, lucidly explain why you do not come out and give a lot of arguments against all that you choose to take. Sometimes this infection is so convincing that you start to believe it, and your head turned on the mechanism of adjustment to the wave of failure, you begin to visit doubt, uncertainty, you become a bystander in this life. But once you talk to a successful person and you will immediately get a lot of arguments for any of your idea, you will find that there are opportunities for all and that you are nothing more than the Joneses, you can achieve just as well as it reached the other. You see, successful people do not know that, why can not they know why it is possible, they install only to win, defeat is simply not accepted, it is not necessary.

You have to hate defeat, though, and be able to play with dignity, which of course will occur in your life, not without it, but you do not have to accept it. Today, you lose, but if you're still alive and breathing, then you're still in this world, and thus the chance to win you have, you can not give up, that is what is the real defeat. Whatever you do not engage, put the task to be the first in this case, may not always be, nor is it important, it is important to prove to yourself that you can be first in everything that you want.

You know what impact this has on your psyche? If not, try it and you will see how you grow up in their own eyes, someone else's opinion you do not need, you can spit at him, think about yourself, how are you going to take, if the blood from his nose, but you have succeeded. While others believe in the impossibility of anything, You are trying to deny it, you can not work, but you, at least, try to do it and I would not be surprised if one of these attempts you will be successful. Also, I would not be surprised if any of successfully completed cases in your life will be more, because the installation of a victory, this is what leads. Play - is not a crime, the real crime is not to believe in their victory, doubt yourself and put up with defeat. You are not born to be content with scraps and do not talk about realistic and sober view because the reality is constantly showing us our limitations. Belief me, the reality can be very different, all that you will implement and reality.

The less you know that you can stop and how this can happen, the less you stop. Installation of winning - it's really something with which we are born, and before we thoroughly wash out the brains, making of us obedient and insecure slaves, we all have the same opportunities. You know that the easiest way to climb over someone is to lower it then drag himself up? So suppressing people psychologically, limiting them primarily through persuasion, we can rise above them, which is what happens in our society. The most talented athlete can be persuaded to defeat, and he would lose, while the weakling, to believe in them, can bypass all.

104

Because, my friends, I do not know whether that defeat or victory, taking place primarily in our heads. You lose, not when someone passes you, and when your mind takes it. I do not know what life has made each one of you, and who you currently are, for me it does not matter, important for me to tell you that the past does not matter, focus on the present and the future, put a goal to win, and Do not think more about. Sport means sports, career, means career, personal life, and social activities, all you need to be the first, the best, the only one of its kind.

Remember - the way to win is not a battle, a war, you can lose many battles, but the war simply have to win. Because only with the installation of winning you have to get up in the morning, saying to myself - now I'm sure of something, but win. And with the thought of winning you have to go to bed. So if you turn the adjustment lever for the victory in his head, a good rope Wrap it in this position, so it is not ever disconnected.